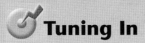

Tuning In

Our Feelings can be read from beginning to end, or it may be more appropriate to read selected sections. Read the introduction *How Do You Feel?*

The front cover

Read the title.

Speaking and Listening

What do you expect to read about in this book?

What feelings can we have?

The back cover

Let's read the blurb together to see if the book is about what we thought.

Contents

Read the list of contents.

Are there any feelings there that we did not think of?

Read pages 2 and 3

Purpose: to read what someone has written about his or her feelings.

Pause at page 3

How many feelings are mentioned in this piece of writing?

What are they?

Are they the same as those listed on the contents page?

Speaking and Listening

What does the author mean by 'think about the ways of dealing with them'?

Look at the words at the top of the page. Which one is a synonym for 'nervous'?

sad   angry   happy   proud   jealous   frightened

How Do You Feel?

My Feelings
I smile when I'm happy.
Mum gets cross when the car won't start.
At first I was jealous of my baby sister, but now I feel proud of her.
I bite my nails when I'm nervous.
I give my friend a hug when he is feeling sad.

We all have different emotions. In this book we will look at some of them and think about the ways of dealing with them.

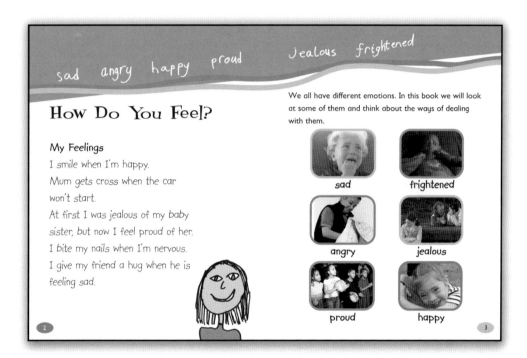

sad

frightened

angry

jealous

proud

happy

READ

Read pages 4 and 5

Purpose: to read about what people do when they are sad.

PAUSE

Pause at page 5

Which of the ideas for cheering yourself up do you use?

Speaking and Listening

Let's read the synonyms across the top of the page.

Do you know any other words for 'sad'?

unhappy   miserable   weepy   gloomy   disappointed   glum

Feeling Sad

When someone is sad they may cry, or go very quiet and put their head in their hands. Most of us feel sad sometimes.

Here are some things you can do to cheer yourself up:
- talk about what has made you sad
- think of something nice
- go for a walk or a run.

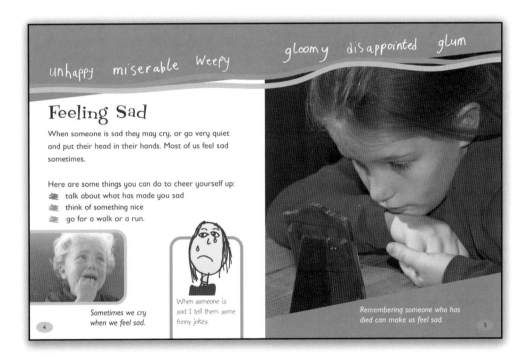

Sometimes we cry when we feel sad.

When someone is sad I tell them some funny jokes.

Remembering someone who has died can make us feel sad.

READ

Read pages 6 and 7

Purpose: to read about how people behave when they are frightened.

PAUSE

Pause at page 7

What has made the boy frightened in the picture?

Speaking and Listening

When is fear a good thing?

Why do people watch really scary films?

Read the synonyms across the top of the page.

Put them in order of the word that means 'least frightened' to 'most frightened'.

alarmed   anxious   scared   terrified   fearful

Feeling Frightened

When you are frightened you might shake or tremble and feel hot and sweaty. Nearly everyone is frightened of something. People might be scared of unknown experiences, or things that they imagine might happen.

Sometimes fear is good because it stops us doing dangerous things. It can also be fun if it's part of a game.

A bad dream can make us feel frightened.

When I'm frightened I think of something nice and feel better.

A rollercoaster ride can be fun **and** scary!

READ

Read pages 8 and 9

Purpose: to find out what people do when they are angry.

PAUSE

Pause at page 9

What does the text say about what to do to make yourself feel better?

Speaking and Listening

Why does moving about or running make some people feel better?

What do you do?

Read the synonyms at the top of the page.

Put them in the order of 'least angry' to 'most angry'.

Do you know another synonym for angry?

cross   annoyed   fuming   mad   furious   irritated

Feeling Angry

When someone is angry they may shout, scream and stamp about. They might feel so angry that they want to explode! Most of us feel angry some of the time.

Moving about or doing something different often helps to stop you feeling angry. Saying 'sorry' and talking to someone can help too.

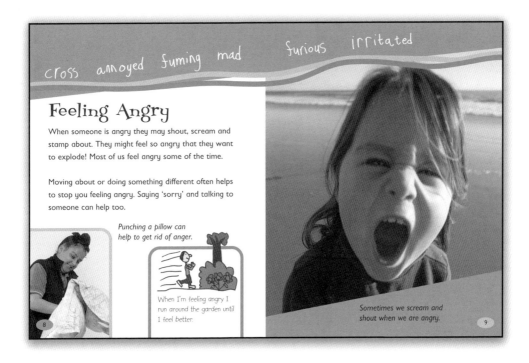

Punching a pillow can help to get rid of anger.

When I'm feeling angry I run around the garden until I feel better.

Sometimes we scream and shout when we are angry.

Read pages 10 and 11

Purpose: to find out how you feel when you are jealous.

Pause at page 11

What does 'sulk' mean?

Speaking and Listening

How do people often behave when they are jealous?

Let's read the synonyms at the top of the page together.

dissatisfied   resentful   envious

Feeling Jealous

You may feel jealous if you are left out of a group, or if someone has something you would like. You may want to sulk and be on your own.

Most people have felt jealous at some time. It helps to think of all the things you do have and that you can do. It also helps to tell someone how you feel.

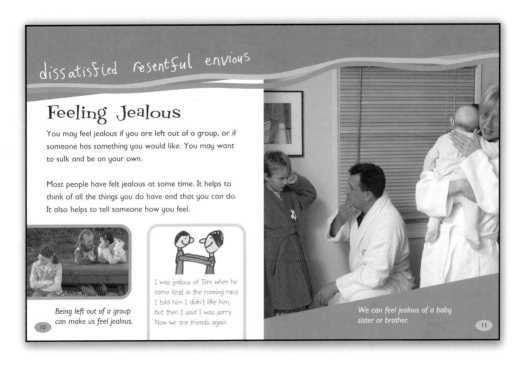

Being left out of a group can make us feel jealous.

I was jealous of Tom when he came first in the running race. I told him I didn't like him, but then I said I was sorry. Now we are friends again.

We can feel jealous of a baby sister or brother.

READ

Read pages 12 and 13

Purpose: to find out when and why people can feel proud.

PAUSE

Pause at page 13

In what ways can we be proud of other people?

Speaking and Listening

Is there a difference between feeling proud and boasting?

Let's read the synonyms at the top of the page.

Which synonym would best describe the way the boy with the cup is feeling?

honoured pleased satisfied   elated contented

Feeling Proud

When someone is feeling proud they stand tall and look very pleased with themselves. They may have worked hard for something and have achieved it at last.

Sometimes we can be proud of ourselves without boasting. We can also be proud of other people.

Winning a prize can make us feel proud.

When I feel proud I hold my head up high.

People often feel proud when they take part in a performance.

READ

Read pages 14 and 15

Purpose: to read about being happy.

PAUSE

Pause at page 15

What would be another feeling that would stop someone feeling happy?

Speaking and Listening

Let's read the synonyms at the top of the page.

What would make you feel thrilled?

Which of those words would you use to describe the pictures?

delighted pleased contented   glad thrilled elated

Feeling Happy

When someone is happy they feel good inside. They may laugh and smile and feel full of energy. Making someone feel happy usually makes you happy too.

Most people don't feel happy all of the time. Sometimes other feelings stop people being happy. Sharing these feelings with others helps us to feel happy more of the time.

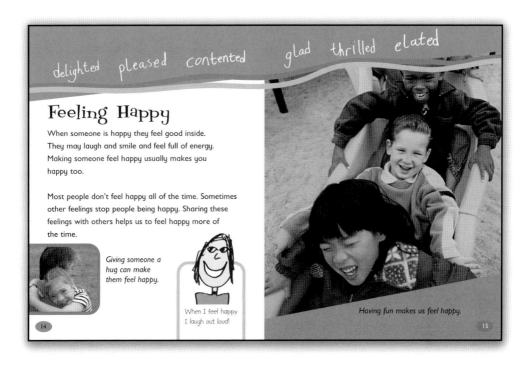

Giving someone a hug can make them feel happy.

When I feel happy I laugh out loud!

Having fun makes us feel happy.

Read page 16

Purpose: to discuss the questions listed.

Pause at page 16

Let's read the list of feelings and how they make us feel together.

Speaking and Listening

Let's think of words to describe how you feel at the different times in the box.

You can flick back through the book and use some of the synonyms to get the best word to describe how you would feel.